ADD & SUBTRACTING

Throughout this book, you will find a whole variety of tests for your child to try with revision guidelines alongside that explain the principles of adding and subtracting.

We recommend that you start by setting your child one of the tests every day. He or she should have a notebook in which to write all the answers. Let him/her work at his/her own pace, but keep a note in the record sheets at the back of this book of how long each exercise takes. Check the answers against those given at the back of this book. Then, if the test is repeated a few weeks later, you can compare both accuracy and speed. You will notice marked improvement.

Encourage your child to practise in this way without using a calculator, and he or she will soon be among those at the top of the class.

ADDING UP — TEST 1

Joe and James share a room. Joe has two pairs of trainers, and his brother, James, has three pairs. How many pairs are there in the cupboard every night if they always put them away?

If you know how to add up, all you need to do is say 2 plus 3 is 5. (You can also write this sum as 2 + 3 = 5.) So there are 5 pairs of trainers in the cupboard each night.

Adding up is not difficult; and if you get lots of practice, you will soon know the answer to a simple sum like 25 + 38 without even thinking about it. (Yes, the answer is 63.)

See if you can do the test on the *right*, the first in this book. There are a lot of numbers to add together in this sum; so if you do not make a mistake, you are doing really well. Even if it takes you a few attempts to get the correct answer, you are still making good progress.

1
add 2
+ 3
add 4
+ 5
add 1
+ 7
+ 8
=

Once you have successfully completed this page, award yourself a star in the box, right.

SETTING OUT   TEST 2

You will often find it easiest to write numbers you need to add up in columns, especially if any of the numbers have two or more figures. You can write out 26 + 13 + 14 = 53 in the following way:

$$\begin{array}{r} 26 \\ 13 \\ +\ 14 \\ \hline 53 \\ \tiny 1 \end{array}$$

The answer goes under the line.

To do this sum, first you add the numbers in the units column on the right (6 + 3 + 4). If this came to 9 or less, you would write this part of the answer under the line in the units column. But it comes to *more* than 9: 13, in fact. So you write down the 3 under the line in the units column on the right and carry over the 1 (one ten) into the tens column to the left of the units column. Now you add up the figures in the tens column (the 1 you carried + 2 + 1 + 1). This comes to 5 and you write the 5 under the line in the tens column, to the left of the 3. So answer the is 53.

	H	T	U
	+		8
+			3
add			2
plus		2	3
+			9
+		3	7
+			5
add			2
=	?	?	?

Note: the column headed H is the hundreds column, T is the tens column and U is the units column.

Once you have correctly completed this test within 60 seconds, award yourself a star.

TEST 3 TEST 4

1 In Philip's money box, there are 5 twenty-pence pieces, 34 pennies, 28 ten-pence pieces and 4 pound coins. How many coins are in the money box?

2 On the top shelf of Gordon's bookcase there are 21 books; on the shelf below, there are 13 books; and on the bottom shelf, 29 books. How many books does Gordon have altogether?

3 On planet Zog, there are some strange animals. Dods have 3 legs each; Mops have 5 legs each; and Bots have 6 legs each. If there are two of each animal in a field, how many legs would there be in that field?

	H	T	U
			2
+		1	8
add			3
plus			7
+		2	5
+		1	0
+			1
add			4
+		1	5
=	?	?	?

Once you have successfully completed this page, award yourself a star in the box, right.

BIG NUMBERS — TEST 5

Adding up is not hard with big numbers either. You just follow the same way of working and prove yourself a genius! Look at 203 + 59 + 118, for example. Again, we can write down the numbers in a column.

```
  263
   59
+ 118
  440
  1 2
```

In this sum, there is a units column (3 + 9 + 8), a tens column (6 + 5 + 1) and a hundreds column (2 + 1).

Starting with the units column, add 3 + 9 + 8. If this came to 9 or less, you could write it under the line in the units column. But it doesn't, does it? It comes to 20. So you write down the 0 under the line in the units column on the right and carry over the 2 to the tens column. Now add the tens column (2 + 6 + 5 + 1) and you will get the answer 14. So, as this is more than 9, put the 4 under the line in the tens column and carry the 1 to the hundreds column. Next you add the hundreds column (1 + 2 + 1) and get the answer 4.

	H	T	U
		1	6
+		2	2
add	2	4	1
plus		1	3
+		1	0
+	2	1	5
+			1
add		1	0
+			1
=	?	?	?

Once you have correctly completed this test within 60 seconds, award yourself a star.

TEST 6

| 4 |
| + 218 |
| add 2 |
| plus 5 |
| + 311 |
| add 7 |
| plus 1 |
| + 28 |
| add 33 |

TEST 7

| 23 |
| plus 4 |
| add 8 |
| + 10 |
| plus 5 |
| + 564 |
| add 12 |
| + 120 |
| + 13 |

Once you have successfully completed this page, award yourself a star in the box, right.

EVEN BIGGER NUMBERS — TEST 8

Now let's try adding really big numbers that have a thousands column: 3473 + 2899. You can set out the sum like this:

```
  3473
+ 2899
  6372
  1 1 1
```

First add 3 + 9 in the units column which equals 12. As this is more than 9, write down the 2 under the line and carry the 1 to the tens column. Now add the tens column (1 + 7 + 9) and you get the answer 17. Write the 7 in the tens column and again carry 1, this time to the hundreds column. Now add the hundreds column (1 + 4 + 8) and you get 13. Write the 3 under the line and carry the 1 to the thousands column. Now add up the thousands column (1 + 3 + 2) and you get 6. Write this under the line in the thousands column. You now have the answer: 6372.

Once you can do this sort of sum without too much bother, you are well on your way to becoming a mathematician!

1 In the number 506, which figure is in the hundreds column?

2 In the number 128, which figure is in the tens column?

3 In the figures 184 and 192, which figures are in the units column?

4 In the numbers 973, 318 and 26, which figures are in the tens column?

5 In the numbers 1380, 5907 and 632, which numbers are in the thousands column?

6 Which number is bigger: 6312 or 4513?

Once you have correctly answered these questions, award yourself a star in the box.

GETTING IT RIGHT — TEST 9

When you read English words, you always start from the left. When you add up columns of numbers, however, you always start at the right with the units column. Then you take one step to the left to the tens column; one step further to the left, if necessary, to the hundreds column; and another step to the left, if necessary, to the thousands column.

When you are adding up big numbers, if the answer in one column is 0 or ends in 0 (20 or 60, perhaps), you need to be sure that you write down any 0 in an answer in the right place under the line. If you are not sure about this, look at this example:

```
   6337
 + 1765
   8102
   1 1 1
```

	H	T	U
	3	0	4
+		2	0
add		7	3
+		1	1
plus	1	4	9
+		3	8
+		4	5
add			9
=	?	?	?

Once you have successfully completed this page within 60 seconds, award yourself a star.

TEST 10　　　TEST 11

	H	T	U
	1	1	3
+		5	2
plus			9
add		3	4
add		1	8
+	5	0	3
plus		2	5
+		6	0
add		9	1
=	?	?	?

a The supermarket opens at 9am. In the first hour, 103 people come in. In the next hour, 397 people come to do their shopping; and between 11am and noon, 428 customers arrive. How many people have been in the shop by midday?

b On the plane to New York, there are 207 people with American passports, 89 people with European passports, 12 with South African passports and 23 with Indian passports. How many people are there on the plane altogether?

c In the car park, there are 312 two-door cars, 416 four-door cars and 68 vans. How many vehicles are there altogether in the car park?

Once you have successfully completed this page, award yourself a star in the box, left.

CHECK IT OUT! TEST 12

When you have an exam or a test at school, if you have time over, it is always a good idea to check your sums. If you do this, you might be able to correct a mistake and get extra marks.

But if you think you have found a mistake, always double-check. Go through it once more, because you might have been right in the first place.

If you need to alter your answer, cross it through with a line, and put the correct answer by the side, above or underneath, wherever it will be clearest.

You need to write neatly because you cannot get marks for something that no one can read!

Never rush your work. It is easy to make a mistake when you hurry.

	H	T	U
	3	0	7
plus	1	5	1
+		3	8
add		9	2
+		2	0
+		1	6
+			4
plus		8	3
add	2	0	6
=	?	?	?

Once you have successfully completed this page, award yourself a star in the box, right.

TAKE IT AWAY! TEST 13

John has 10 marbles and he gives James 4. How many marbles does John have left?

All you have to do with this sum is take away 4 marbles from 10 marbles. You can say 10 subtract 4, or 10 minus 4, or 10-4, or 10 take away 4. The answer is, of course, 6. (When you were smaller, you probably used to do this sort of sum using your fingers. If you want to do this sometimes, you still can. But with practice, you will find you can easily do this sort of sum in your head.)

We can also write out this sum like this:

$$\begin{array}{r} 10 \\ -\ 4 \\ \hline 6 \end{array}$$

Look carefully at the wording of the sums in TEST 13. Subtract 1 from 7, remember, means the same as 7 take away 1 or 7-1, or 7 minus 1.

a. From 10 take away 5.

b. From 4 take away 3.

c. From 9 subtract 5.

d. 8 - 4

e. Subtract 8 from 9.

f. 4 - 0

g. Subtract 1 from 7.

h. 8 minus 3.

Once you have successfully completed this page within 60 seconds, award yourself a star.

LARGE NUMBERS TEST 14

If you have to do a subtraction sum with bigger numbers (perhaps 68-59, for example), you can set it out like this:

$$\begin{array}{r} 68 \\ -\ 55 \\ \hline 13 \end{array}$$

Just as you do when you are adding up, you have to start on the right in the units column. Say 8 take away 5, and you get 3. Write down the 3 under the line in the units column. Now move to the tens column. Yes, that's it: you go to the left. Say 6 take away 5, and you get 1. Write down the 1 under the line in the tens column. Now you have the answer written under the line : it is 13.

Try TEST 14 and see if you can get them all right!

a. From 15 take away 11.

b. 25 - 5

c. 42 - 31

d. 83 - 52

e. Subtract 27 from 38.

f. 48 - 22

g. Subtract 23 from 34.

h. 76 - 44

Once you have correctly answered these questions, award yourself a star in the box.

BORROWING TEN   TEST 15

Sometimes when you are doing a subtraction sum, you will need to borrow from the tens column. Look at the following example.

$$\begin{array}{r}67\\-39\\\hline 28\end{array}$$

As usual, you start with the units column. You cannot take 9 from 7, however, because 9 is bigger than 7. So you borrow from the tens column and turn the 7 into 17 by writing a little 1 at the side of it. At the same time, you turn the 6 in the tens column into a 5 because you have borrowed 1 from it to create the 17. Now say 17 take away 9 = 8, and write down 8 in the units column under the line. Next go to the tens column and say 5 - 3 = 2. Write the 2 under the line in the tens column. You now have the answer: it is 28.

a. 63 - 48

b. 52 - 39

c. Subtract 17 from 45.

d. 38 minus 29

e. Subtract 36 from 91.

f. 73 - 27

g. 93 - 48

Once you have successfully completed this page, award yourself a star in the box, left.

MORE BORROWING   TEST 16

Look at this example:

```
  124
-  38
   86
```

Starting in the units column, you cannot take 8 from 4 because 8 is bigger than 4. So you borrow 1 ten from the tens column and turn the 4 into 14 by putting the borrowed 1 in front of it. At the same time, you turn the 2 in the tens column to 1 because you borrowed one ten from it. Now say 14 – 8 = 6, and write the 6 under the line in the units column.

Next look at the tens column. You cannot take 3 from 1 because 3 is bigger than 1. So you now have to borrow from the hundreds column. When you do this, you turn the new 1 in the tens column into 11. At the same time, you turn the 1 in the hundreds column to 0 because of what you have borrowed. Now say 11 – 3 = 8 and write down the 8 under the line in the tens column. In this sum, there will be nothing in the hundreds column because 0 take away nothing is nought. So the answer is 86.

a. 158 - 37

b. 504 - 28

c. 629 minus 84

d. From 527 subtract 39

e. Take away 147 from 312

f. 284 - 57

g. From 973 take away 129

Once you have successfully completed this page, award yourself a star in the box, right.

BREAK

All the practice you are getting in adding and subtracting should help with these.

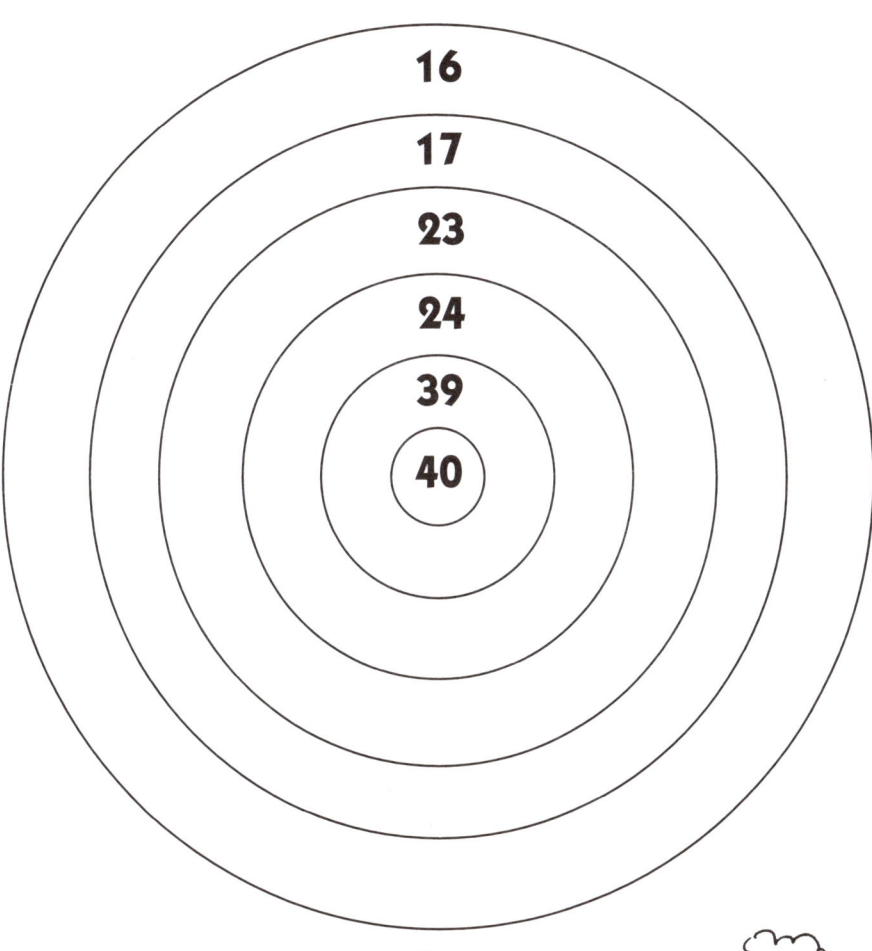

Target rings (outer to inner): 16, 17, 23, 24, 39, 40

Paul was given an unusual darts game for Christmas. It comes with a series of challenges. One of these is to reach a score of 100 by throwing 5 darts. How can he do this? In another challenge, he has to get a score of 119 with only 3 darts. How can he do that?

TEST 19   TEST 20

a In a cinema, there are 16 people in row A, 22 people in row B, 14 in row C, 18 in row D, 19 in row E and 21 in row F. The rest of the cinema is empty. How many people are there in the cinema together?

b Sixty-four of the people in the cinema buy an ice cream. How many do not buy an ice cream?

c After the film, 20 people go home by car, 12 go by bus and the rest go by train. How many go by train?

d Half of those who saw the film liked it. How many did not like the film?

160

plus 29

- 0

add 14

+ 136

minus 24

minus 83

plus 492

take away 39

Once you have correctly answered this page within 90 seconds, award yourself a star.

TEST 21

1
A shopkeeper wants to see how much he needs to order for his shop. He always likes to stock tins of sardines but only has 54 on the shelf instead of 100. He likes to have 200 packets of tea, but there are only 94. There should also be 150 jars of jam but he only has 81.
How many
a. tins of sardines
b. packets of tea
c. jars of jam
should he order?

2
If a man walks 5 miles north, 3 miles east, 1 mile west and 2 miles south, how far will he walk in total if he goes back by the same route?

TEST 22

1001

+ 279

- 356

plus 4

minus 23

add 149

take away 12

+ 24

minus 32

Once you have successfully completed this page, award yourself a star in the box, left.

TEST 23

| 160 |
| + 32 |
| − 98 |
| +14 |
| plus 83 |
| minus 22 |
| + 64 |
| add 31 |
| + 79 |

TEST 24

a If there are 15 flats on the ground floor, 18 flats on the first floor, 30 flats on the second floor and 20 flats on the third floor, how many flats are there in the block altogether?

b 84 children leave a primary school at the end of term and 73 new pupils join. There were 412 in the school to start with. How many will be there next term?

c The party table is full with sandwiches of four kinds. On one plate, there are 18 ham sandwiches; on another, 10 egg sandwiches; on another, 12 cheese sandwiches; and on another, 14 tuna sandwiches. How many sandwiches are on the table altogether?

Once you have successfully completed this page, award yourself a star in the box, right.

TEST 25

a. 732 + 536

b. 804 + 799

c. 36 - 27

d. 22 + 0 + 470

e. 56 + 32 + 84

f. 63 - 29 - 15

g. 181 - 97 - 36

h. 110 - 11 - 47

i. 68 + 3 + 12

TEST 26

173

add 68

take away 22

+ 339

- 482

plus 512

+ 64

minus 18

+73

Once you have correctly answered these questions, award yourself a star in the box.

TEST 27

a At the bank, they are counting up money. In one bag, there are 500 £1 coins. In another, there are 182, in another, 370, and in another, 148. How much money is there altogether?

b Anne has £87 in the bank. On Monday, she puts in £22. On Tuesday, she takes out £41. On Wednesday, she puts in £53, and on Thursday, she takes out £15. How much does she have in the bank at the end of Thursday?

c Mary is collecting books so that she can sell them for charity. Rod gives her 16 books, Penny gives her 19 books, Julie gives her 11 books and Robin gives her 18 books. How many books has Mary so far?

TEST 28

47

− 13

+ 183

add 19

− 22

+ 37

+ 252

− 10

plus 69

Once you have successfully completed this page, award yourself a star in the box, right.

TEST 29

a Jane spent 30 minutes doing her homework on Friday evening, 45 minutes on Saturday and 55 minutes on Sunday. How long did it take her altogether, in minutes?

b Bobby said he would meet Jim at the station at 11.10am but he was 15 minutes late. What time did he get there?

c A shoe shop has 387 pairs in sizes 3, 4 and 5. 49 pairs are in size 3 and 112 pairs are in size 4. How many pairs are in size 5?

TEST 30

1

+ 111

+ 191

- 61

+101

take away 11

+ 13

minus 215

plus 131

Once you have correctly answered this page within 90 seconds, award yourself a star.

TEST 31

a. 63 + 24 + 108

b. 79 + 4 + 15

c. 419 + 23 + 18

d. 103 - 44 - 8

e. 37 + 93 + 24

f. 182 - 9 - 3

g. 704 - 192 - 8

h. 63 + 71 + 5

i. 82 + 0 + 54

TEST 32

a. John is looking forward to his holiday in 12 days' time. If today is 14 March, on which day does he go on holiday?

b. If today is 30 July and Peter broke up from school 9 days ago, which day was the last day of term?

c. Polly lives at number 1 in her street. On her side, the numbers are all odd and run 1, 3, 5, 7, 9 and so on. On the other side, however, the numbers are all even and run 2, 4, 6, 8 and so on. Her best friend lives 10 houses away from Polly. At which number does she live?

Once you have successfully completed this page, award yourself a star in the box, right.

TEST 33

83

− 72

+ 118

− 21

minus 38

plus 243

minus 29

+ 94

TEST 34

1 Rosie usually sleeps for 10 hours. If she goes to bed at 8pm, at what time does she wake up?

2 On Tuesday, Rosie went to bed at 8pm as usual, but woke at 1am and could not get back to sleep for an hour. If she slept 11 hours that night, at what time did she get up?

3 Robin is Rosie's little brother and he usually goes to bed at 7pm. If he sleeps for 12 hours, at what time does he generally wake up?

4 If I borrow 8 books from the library on Monday, take back 3 on Tuesday, and take back 4 on Thursday, how many have I still got?

Once you have correctly answered this page within 90 seconds, award yourself a star.

TEST 35

a. 590 + 483

b. 672 + 711

c. 98 - 49

d. 33 + 98 + 114

e. 63 + 84 + 92

f. 111 - 52 - 38

g. 712 - 99 - 34

h. 622 - 47 - 18

i. 92 + 74 + 118

TEST 36

312

-99

add 47

- 32

+ 115

- 74

+ 83

+ 570

- 24

Once you have correctly answered these questions, award yourself a star in the box.

TEST 37   TEST 38

a
There are 360 passengers on a ship. 49 get off at Athens, and another 27 at Haifa. How many passengers will then be left to continue the cruise?

712

- 518

+ 36

b
Jack has a huge box of chocolates and the packet says it contains 68 in all. On Saturday, he gives his mother 2, and eats 3 himself. On Sunday, he eats 2 and gives his friend 4. Later in the day, he gives his grandmother four, too. How many does he now have left?

plus 91

- 34

+ 87

- 101

c
The book that Freddie is reading has 106 pages. He has read 81 so far. How many pages are there left to read?

+ 14

add 28

Once you have successfully completed this page, award yourself a star in the box, left.

TEST 39

a. If there are 1,480 people at a football match, and 365 are under 16, how many are 16 or over?

b. In the imaginary land of Skip, there are 5,740 men, 6,212 women and 3,110 children. What is the total population of the land of Skip?

c. Disaster! There were 540 eggs on the supermarket shelf but it collapsed and 318 broke. How many were left?

d. At the disco, Lucy danced 3 times with Harry, 4 times with Oliver and 6 times with Colin. How many times did she dance altogether?

TEST 40

a. 61 + 99

b. 133 + 42 + 8

c. 173 + 99 + 24

d. 293 + 84 + 68

e. 27 + 183 + 98

f. 37 + 12 + 149

g. 136 - 10 - 27

h. 83 + 82 + 81

i. 67 - 12 - 18

Once you have successfully completed this page, award yourself a star in the box, right.

RECORD SHEET

DATE	TEST	SCORE ✓ OR X	TIME
1.2.00	ONE	2½m X 2m15 X	2½ 2.

RECORD SHEET

DATE	TEST	SCORE ✓ OR X	TIME

ANSWERS

TEST 1
31

TEST 2
89

TEST 3
a. 71 b. 63 c. 28

TEST 4
85

TEST 5
629

TEST 6
609

TEST 7
759

TEST 8
1. 5 2. 2 3. 4, 2
4. 7, 1, 2 5. 1, 5
6. 6312

TEST 9
649

TEST 10
905

TEST 11
a. 928 b. 331 c. 796

TEST 12
917

TEST 13
a. 5 b. 1 c. 4 d. 4
e. 1 f. 4 g. 6 h. 5

TEST 14
a. 4 b. 20 c. 11 d. 31
e. 11 f. 26 g. 11
h. 32

TEST 15
a. 15 b. 13 c. 28 d. 9
e. 55 f. 46 g. 45

TEST 16
a. 121 b. 476 c. 545
d. 488 e. 165 f. 227
g. 844

TEST 17
410

TEST 18
a. 131 b. 67 c. 154
d. 1581 e. 275 f. 55
g. 459 h. 158 i. 263

TEST 19
a. 110 b. 46 c. 78
d. 55

TEST 20
685

TEST 21
1. a. 46 b. 106 c. 69
2. 22 miles

TEST 22
1034

TEST 23
343

TEST 24
a. 83 b. 401 c. 54

TEST 25
a. 1268 b. 1603 c. 9
d. 492 e. 172 f. 19
g. 48 h. 52 i. 83

TEST 26
707

TEST 27
a. £1,200 b. £106
c. 64

TEST 28
562

TEST 29
a. 130 b. 11.25am
c. 226

TEST 30
261

TEST 31
a. 195 b. 98 c. 460
d. 51 e. 154 f. 170
g. 504 h. 139 i. 136

TEST 32
a. 26 March
b. 21 July c. 21

TEST 33
378

TEST 34
1. 6am 2. 8am
3. 7am 4. 1

TEST 35
a. 1073 b. 1383 c. 49
d. 245 e. 239 f. 21
g. 579 h. 557 i. 284

TEST 36
898

TEST 37
a. 284 b. 53 c. 25

TEST 38
315

TEST 39
a. 1,115 b. 15,062
c. 222 d. 13

TEST 40
a. 160 b. 183 c. 296
d. 445 e. 308 f. 198
g. 99 h. 246 i. 37

TAKE A BREAK
c
3 darts in ring 16 (48),
1 dart in ring 29 (29),
1 dart in ring 23 (23),
= 100; 2 darts in ring
40 (80), 1 dart in ring
39 (39), = 119

Published by
Arcturus Publishing Limited
for Index Books
Henson Way
Kettering
Northamptonshire
NN16 8PX

ISBN 1-900032-94-5

This edition published 2000

All rights reserved. No part of
this publication may be reproduced,
stored in a retrieval system, or transmitted
in any form or by any means, electronic,
mechanical, photocopying, recording or
otherwise, without written
permission or in
accordance with the
Copyright Act 1956 (as ammended).
Any person or persons who do any
unauthorised act in relation to this publication
may be liable to criminal prosecution and
civil claims for damages

Printed in Italy

© Arcturus Publishing Limited
1-7 Shand Street
London
SE1 2ES

Created by Quartz Editions
Edited by Anne Fennell